# FOOLISH INVESTOR WISE INVESTOR

# A JOURNEY OF FINANCIAL MASTERY

## BY

## ONUORAH MICHAEL WILLIAMS
### (michaelwilliams0545@yahoo.com)

I0407778

# INTRODUCTION

This book is not just a recounting of financial triumphs and tribulations; it's a roadmap for readers of all backgrounds and levels of financial expertise. Whether you're a seasoned investor looking to refine your approach or a novice seeking guidance, the pages that follow hold invaluable insights into the art and science of making sound investment decisions.

The book contains the story of a young and eager investor who starts his journey with boundless enthusiasm but minimal knowledge. As he navigates the treacherous waters of the stock market, he makes every mistake in the book. From chasing hot trends to falling for get-rich-quick schemes, he found himself mired in the depths of financial missteps and costly mistakes, From impulsive stock picks to following the crowd without question.

Through it all, "Once a Foolish Investor Who Later Became a Wise Investor" offers invaluable lessons for both novice and seasoned investors. You'll discover the secrets to identifying sound investment opportunities, managing risks, and achieving financial independence. It's a thrilling narrative that will leave you not only entertained but also empowered to take control of your own financial destiny.

If you've ever felt the sting of a bad investment or dreamed of building wealth through savvy financial choices, this book is your roadmap to success. With wit, humor, and a healthy dose of self-deprecation, the once-foolish investor will inspire you to transform your own financial future. Don't miss out on this captivating story of redemption and financial mastery. Dive in today and start your journey from foolish to fabulous!

## WISE INVESTOR INTRODUCTION:

The first thing you need to bear in mind is that investment and trading are equal to gambling, Before you choose to go into trading and investment keep in mind that you need to know the truth and rules, you need to prepare your mind for the worst in as much you enjoy the benefits, you need to prepare your mind to learn, you need to prepare your heart against emotions. Trading is not just what you can feel you know or think you know rather trading is a consequential practice. You don't trade with emotions, you don't trade with guesses, you don't trade with sentiment rather you practice and learn to trade. There are a lot of ups and downs when it comes to trading and investment you need to know. So as a newbie in trading and investment space, you don't just dive into the system with a greedy heart. I was continuously and easily scammed because of my greedy heart to make it easier, quicker, and bigger even without knowing the basic dynamics and rules of trading even to the detriment of sacrificing all my hard-earned savings foolishly. There are wrongs factors you need first to exclude before going into trading and investing, these wrong factors can easily cripple your finances or quickly liquidate your trading capital, during my long years of bitter experiences I have learned the hard way to know these wrong factors as; Lack of technical knowhow known as Knowledge, Greed, Wrong Mindset, Frustration, and Emotions,

**Lack of technical Knowhow;** When I use the word lack of technical knowhow I literally mean not having adequate knowledge of what you are going into or what you are doing at that time, going into trading and investment but having little or no technical knowhow (Knowledge) or without having a knowledgeable human guidance will cause you to make huge unforgettable mistakes in the financial market. This was my own worst scenario jumping into the financial market having only little knowledge of it that I learnt on YouTube and I felt I have known the market fair enough to trade and do investing on my own but I totally lost it all. I strongly advise if you don't have a good knowledge of trading and investing don't be too quick to entrust your money to any trading platform least you have prepared to lose it all, You need to have a good knowledge of the market, or you need to have someone as a guardian who his testament has proven good results over the years in the financial market. Learning it by yourself on social media is not good enough to go full-time trading by yourself unless you are prepared to bear the loss over and over again. Trading is too profitable and at the same time too risky to dabble into it without having the techniques and market analysis to trade, you need to know the fundamental and technical analysis, talking from my own mistake, I am quick to engage in trading with the basic fundamental analysis I learned from the internet without knowing the most needed technical analysis. Again, before you plan to put your money in with any financial brokers or exchange Apps, do your findings very well, Don't be deceived by people's sentiments or any sort of online testifiers about any trading and investment site or App. most sites and Apps are just phishing baits looking for your hard-earned money to be trapped in their account. Don't be carried away with the pictures they paint to be true rather do your diligent research about the broker, the site, or the App, ask questions don't be too eager or carried away by many bloggers' posts on the internet about a particular financial brooker, trading App, stock or token because they are paid for it to hype and do the bidders marketing, the bloggers are only doing their business to survive, always check on the disclaimer, check on people comment, ask deeper questions and do your own adequate research.

**EMOTION:** Don't allow or bring your emotion into the financial market, your emotion can cripple your money, so take away your emotion In trading, never trade with your emotion or judge a particular stock, token, or financial brokers with your emotion. In as much as your instinct might be right in most cases don't bring it into the financial market system because it will fail you in that aspect. I was a victim of this by judging the market with my instincts which led me to make so many wrong choices because I allowed my emotion to cloud my sense of human logical reasoning. Most times that I allowed my emotion to rule my judgment on a particular broker, token, or stock I always fail woefully. Take away your emotions when trading. Your instinct can tell you that a particular token or stock is doing well in the market not knowing is just a hype stock or pump and dumb coin, By the time you eventually invest your money into that stock or token you will watch your money crash to zero. Don't trade or invest with your instinct rather do it with knowledge and experience.

**WRONG MINDSET:** This factor can also contribute to the wrong factors that hinder trading and investing. At first in my own scenario as a case study what really drives me into the financial market unprepared is because of my wrong earlier motive or mindset of "Sleep, wake, and see money" without working anything". I was too quick to make it in trading and investing, I was too eager to start cashing it big and doing nothing, and I was too quick to be in the line of getting quick money and that was the ultimate reason why I blindly stumble into the financial market. Because for me the mindset I use in coming into the market in the early year of 2016 was to invest my money with any financial brokers and relax as I watch my money grow every day in greater profit without doing any work, so that wrong mindset cripple my right mind as I began to fall from one scam to another continuously with the same wrong mindset of getting it back my lost money bigger. I didn't enter the financial market with the right mindset that trading and investing is what I would love to do, or I didn't think in another way that trading and investing is spare little money that will be useful in the near future. I only have the mindset of getting rich-quick syndrome, being lazy, and doing nothing but seeing money flying into my bank account. I didn't see trading and investing from a standpoint as strictly business rather I entered the market system to satisfy my lazy wish of "Sleep, wake up, and see money but practically not doing anything. So my advice to you is never to enter the financial market with the wrong motive.

**FRUSTRATION:** Trading in the financial market with a mix of Frustration in your mind will make you lose and lose over and over again in the market. You feel frustrated when the market is turning against your position, you feel frustrated entering the market because of your previous loss, you feel frustrated because of the weaken day news about the financial market, and you feel frustrated that you are not getting the expected profit you want, you feel frustrated because you see others on social media in the internet who becomes a millionaire in trading and investment meanwhile in your case there is nothing to show that you will make it big like those you read and watch on the internet, you wish to become like Warren Buffet and other great investors and traders, you feel frustrated of what will be the outcome of your investment. Your frustration can greatly affect your trading in the financial market and equally affect your life generally by driving you into depression, anger, and anxiety. So keep away frustration in the financial market.

**GREED:** The last to discuss is greed. This is one of the most deadly factors among all that have affected so many traders and investors negatively, the explanation of greed is enormous. Greed has caused many not to know how to take a limit that can reduce trading risk. The greed of wanting to gain it big by all costs, the greed of wanting to earn big with little capital investment, the greed of wanting it now and not next time, greed has caused me a lot to lose so much money in the financial market. Trade and invest with caution, don't invest or trade with all your savings don't invest or trade with a bank loan, don't borrow money from family or friends, and don't sell your valuable property to invest or trade. Most of the time greed and lust cause us to do things that we blindly blame on passion.

A word is enough for the wise, all that is written down in this book is a testament to my experience in the financial market, I made so many mistakes that out of my sincere heart I wouldn't like anyone to make the same mistake, learn from my rough mistake which I have learned in a hard way. You can smartly avoid making such mistakes as I have done by reading carefully and applying to it. The book though centered on trading and investing in the financial market is equally a general advice and lesson to all in all ramifications of life. Carefully Journey with me to my story lane and learn one or two things from my foolish mistakes. Information is key, Information is one of the necessary tool you need in life to succeed efficiently, Learn from the information in this book apply it.

## THE THOUGHT OF "SLEEP, WAKE UP AND SEE MONEY" (THE BIRTH OF ALL)

As far back in the year 2010 driving it down my memory lane, I was living in a town called Awka known as the capital city of old Anambra State, Nigeria. I was living together with a family friend named Sunday nicknamed (But Why). Sunday though been older than me in age but at times reasons with me as though we are at the same level of age.

I and Sunday always lived in our fool paradise with the dream of one significant thing which was "Sleep, wake up, and see money" without working or doing anything in life. We seriously conceive this fantasy lifestyle as though if we were kids because kids are always known to think freely and at times foolishly unimaginable fantasy known as fool paradise. On second thought I will also say that we have time to regularly conceive such thoughts because we lack something to do. We both are doing nothing at that time that can engage our minds and keep them busy rather at that time what we know how to do best is to only sleep, wake up, eat, chat, and watch television which gives us the privilege to start wishing for such permanent lifestyle but impossible to happen, the daily continuation of our jobless lazy lifestyle. Because of our daily wishing to live the life of "Sleep, wake up, eat, watch TV or play music and do nothing but still see money coming into the bank account we began to formularize our lifestyle to be that way not knowing that life is all about laws. The universe is guided by laws of input and output system of sowing and reaping. But as it is said, guide your thoughts that enter into the subconscious mind which has the power to transmute either negative or positive manifestations, then our thought of "Sleep, wake up and see money" becloud our mentality and vision that we don't think anything further on how to work and make the dream manifest to reality, we don't have plans on how to make our childish fantasy of 'Sleep, wake up and see money' to becomes a reality. I remember vividly that we didn't just end it only thinking it in our minds to happen but we began to confess it to the ears of all those who gave us a listening ear to our confession. Then, when one asked us what is our aspirations in life we would boldly reply to you that we want a life of "Sleep, wake up and see money but working nothing" as though it were kids talking. But the power of thought was really taking control of us unknowingly for us, that we imagine it, confess it, and to the point exhibit it through laziness. The thought of doing nothing but seeing money and living a comfortable life crippled our ability to work and drives us into a lazy state of mind, lazy adults because we wish for good life and want not to work anymore but enjoy the goodies of life because we constantly believe in the reality of doing nothing or less stress but still has cash flow. At a very young age in life, I was busy thinking of the retirement stage where I would relax doing nothing any more but "Sleep, wake up, and see money" when I did not even plan to work out for the life that I desired for myself. I was making a wish to the universe without being careful of what I was wishing for.

## WISE INVESTOR

First, I would say that the thought I have for myself of "Sleep, wake up, and see money is not really a bad idea but what I fail to understand is that it is a plan to make for the future after I must have to work it out in my young age in preparation for retirement stage in life, but first squarely face the reality of life by working it out hard and smart in my young stage of life in prepare of the future retirement stage so that I can be able to live the kind of life I wish for after I must have gathered the investment that will aid me to live to the very status of life. I was too quick to wish for a good thing in my future to come but I allow the thought to becloud my mental reasoning and crippled my mindset that what I consistently wish then is for the thought to start playing immediately at my current stage as a young boy when I have not practically done anything to work towards such dream. 'Sleep, wake up, and see money is a good thought for a retirement plan in life and not at the early stage of life when you are still building the foundation of your life.

Having such thought is good but working towards such thought to actualize the dream is the best.

Secondly, it is never advisable to be idle, for it is said that an idle mind is a free devil workshop. A busy person will hardly have the time to nurture impossible fantasies in his heart, An idle mind encourages laziness, it encourages conceiving many negative thoughts and less positive thoughts, Thought is free, and you can think to the extent you want without being charged for it. Thought is good only when thinking of something that can be transformed into something beneficial. Thought is a powerful tool that can make a future or mar a future so it is advisable to be very careful of what you think and wish for. I believe in my own scenario of life that what I continually gave time to think about begins to cripple me. At first, the thought of "Sleep, wake up and see money" started as a joke but the effectual continually thinking of such an impossible fantasy entered into my subconscious mind that I began to confess it to others and lastly desiring it to happen too quickly in my life. Always be careful with the kind of thoughts and decisions you are making in life. I was too quick to retire and begin to enjoy life even when I did not work for the kind of life I wish for myself, I assure you that thoughts are powerful striking tools that have the effectual power to affect whatever thing about you negatively or positively but I will advise you to always think positively in whatsoever you are doing in life.

## 2014 THE NEWS ABOUT BITCOIN, THE FIRST CRYPTOCURRENCY

All moment after conceiving the thought of 'Sleep, wake and see money" the thought residually became part of me that what I want in life is "Sleep, wake up and see money" Ever since then I never knew how to apply the chemistry that will produce the result of what I constantly desired but though I still wish for it to happen in my life just as I have always dream.
Journey to the year 2014 which was my final year in a higher institution, A departmental friend named Kinsley gave a seminar topic on Bitcoin and that was my very first year hearing about a crypto currency called Bitcoin. Then he explains that Bitcoin is the new digital currency that will replace fiat soon. He further explains that a little portion of Bitcoin you buy now can make you rich tomorrow even when you don't work for it. The statement he made of buying a little portion of Bitcoin now and becoming rich tomorrow stuck in my head, I became interested to hear more and to really understand this new digital currency so well and how it works because this has always been my dream of not working hard or at all but still be rich (The theory of "Sleep, wake and see money") I further ask him questions on Bitcoin, which he explain though not too expounded, but I remembered him

saying that you can buy a little portion of Bitcoin with few dollars and hold it in your digital wallet in a long run it has the possibility to turn into thousands of dollars if the coin appreciates in market value. I asked him again if I have to work or do anything that will assist the coin to appreciate in market value but he answered and said no that all I have to do is to buy and hold in my wallet and watch my coin appreciate in value whenever the market goes up. In my head I said This is it, this is what I have been looking for all the while, this is my dream since 2010 of "Sleep, wake up and see money" trying to come into reality. That very day after the seminar my thought was all about Bitcoin, thoughts on where will I start, and how to buy this coin that would aid my dream to come true, I remembered meeting with Kingsley on several occasions trying to get the answer that I needed about Bitcoin and how to buy a little portion of the coin with my little school pocket money, because to me I just needed what will be generating money for me even when I am sleeping or not working for it. Unfortunately, I didn't get the actual answer I wanted from Kingsley on how to buy the coin because he wasn't too sure of the means of purchasing the coin, he told me he only knew about the theory of Bitcoin existence but has not purchased the coin, that a friend of his only heard it from someone else who told him about the new digital coin trending and making people big in the area of finance. All my effort trying to source a means of buying the coin proved abortive till we graduated from school and we parted ways, My burning desire to secure the new era currency was quenched because I didn't see anyone to support the high spirit I had in me concerning Bitcoin. Kingsely that have the same spirit as me is no longer within my reach to put me through and gear my spirit up for I solely depend on Kingsely's knowledge about the new era coin known as Bitcoin.


**WISE INVESTOR OBSERVATION:**
Obviously, I have the passion to purchase a little portion of Bitcoin not minding sacrificing from my little school pocket money but my weakness and the huge mistake I made was that I solely depended on Kingsely's knowledge about Bitcoin, I failed to research deeply on my own of how to go about it and buy Bitcoin because as of 2014 we are already in the era of the internet age and there are already a lot of trusted Crypto Exchange App where I could have traded Bitcoin, but I fail to understand this because I was too lazy in the brain but I dream to be rich in the mind. Kingsely's seminar let me know an important information I didn't know about before but I failed to work with the information because I settled it in my mind that since Kingsley is the guy with the information he was supposed to know everything about Bitcoin and how to buy Bitcoin and since he fails to know

the whole information It means it is an impossible or too big thing to do meanwhile buying crypto as of then is just too simple, the very mistake I made was relying or limiting my knowledge on Kingsley knowledge, I fail to know that what he Kingsley was limited to know that I can strive to make deeper research farther to know more than the limit he knows. That is the problem of most people in real life, They rely on limited people's knowledge, government knowledge, media knowledge, religious leaders' knowledge, political leader's knowledge, and parent and school teacher's knowledge and never bother to strive to seek deeper knowledge above what they are been told or taught. The truth was that an early purchase of Bitcoin would have been my partial dream accomplishment of "Sleep, wake and see money" assuming I never gave up on how to buy a portion of Bitcoin. As of the year 2014, Bitcoin was still in its early development and acceptance stage in the global market meaning that the price has not gone up as of its current trading price now, The closing price of Bitcoin in the year 2014 on December 31, was three hundred and eighteen dollars $318. So I really believe that if assuming I bought $100 or $200 worth of Bitcoin in the year 2014 I would have been cashing out thousands of dollars in a few years to come just as Kingsley earlier explained because, in the year November 2021, Bitcoin hit to it all-time high giving a market value of sixty-five thousand dollars $65,000. No one would have ever thought that a tiny unknown token called Bitcoin would have hit its peak as it did in the year 2021. So I will say I messed up my dream of "Sleep, waking up, and seeing money" because I gave up on Bitcoin. Most times real things or rather will I say informative opportunities that can change life don't come repeatedly knocking at the door for long, it is always better to work with a well-presented opportunity at that available time it comes knocking. This will be financial advice to everyone, whether young or old, student, worker or business person but most especially the young ones in school, learn to build a future investment in stocks, as you are growing in life grow with your portfolio of little or much investment in stocks or whichever asset you can buy don't eat away all your pocket money, don't waste much of your money buying school materials because after school there is no guarantee for you that you will be rich rather you are enriching your lecturer or school proprietor pocket. I beat my hand in my chest and proudly advise you to limit wasting so much money on school materials, practical's, or whatever means that school uses to keep siphoning money from you. As a student, it earlier better in your early year one to create an investment portfolio and start buying stocks no matter how little you can afford, It will surprise you to see how far your investment will have grown after graduation from school, and then the money can be your fall back plan to start life after school, you can buy a tangible asset with the money or rather still it will serve as a capital fund for you to start a business and not hoping and waiting for the government or for any firm to secure a job. This is what I and most of my school mate fail to do because we lack financial knowledge, we didn't come across someone who would help enlighten us with financial knowledge for what only preoccupied our mentality was study hard get the best grade, graduate, and get employed by any of the best company, no lecturer from my year one to my final year ever taught us the principles of investment and financial knowledge, but just as Robert said in his book Rich Dad Poor Dad, that the teacher will not teach what they themselves fail to know or don't have the knowledge about. I and most of my school mate made this mistake but I wouldn't like any young student in college to repeat the same mistake we made, It is never too late to start now in case you are thinking that you already graduated from higher institution and now working you can equally start now and build a financial back up by creating an investment portfolio. You might be wondering how to grow your asset portfolio you can simply do that by giving yourself a task of investing ten or twenty percent of your daily, weekly, or monthly income into an asset that has the potential of appreciating in the long run. Having savings is so important but also build an investment portfolio. Don't only save all your money in a bank because your money can never grow in your bank savings account, and also don't invest all your savings money in stock you only invest with some percent of your money to mitigate risks that come with it. I missed the opportunity to invest in Bitcoin early in the year the coin was selling for three hundred dollars per Bitcoin; I regretted it till today of not investing on time. This advice is mostly for the young ones who are still in higher intuition, School will never teach you about finance just as Robert said in his book Rich Dad and Poor Dad, but that is simply the truth. All school will encode in your mind is graduate and look for a job. During my time in school, I was never taught about investing and how to build wealth; rather it was just graduate and look for a job. As a young student the earlier you start now building your investment portfolio the better for you in the short future.

Research on potential stock to buy, I failed to continue to research further on how to buy Bitcoin in 2014 after hearing the information from Kingsely, We graduated from school and the sight of not seeing Kingsely again kills the burning desire that was earlier in me to purchase a little portion of Bitcoin. I have to learn it the hard way that my destiny is not tied to someone else, most times you don't just need someone else to be part of the thing you can do for yourself before you do it. The thought that Kingsely was no longer with me to help me purchase Bitcoin kills my passion for buying Bitcoin earlier and that was how I missed the opportunity, assuming I press forward that I never rely on Kingsely's limited knowledge on Bitcoin and press further on researching by myself probably I wouldn't have missed the chance to purchase Bitcoin earlier stage then.

## 2016 MY FIRST BUSINESS SUMMIT SEMINAR (BSS)

After I graduated from college, just as always school has encoded in my brain to graduate and look for a job. At that year 2015, I was out of school and launched myself into the labor market, I drafted my CV and started applying for a job from one firm to another submitting my CV online and offline, At this very time nobody preached to me to shun off the lazy believe concerning my mentality of "Sleep, wake up and see money" But I noticed the mentality flew away from me when I really face the reality of life, knowing too well that I needed money to pay bills and take care of myself, no more free money or sponsorship money from my father, I am now to take care of my responsibilities. I now needed to work out for my money, though I never still liked the idea of working too hard to earn little, I buried my thoughts of sleep, waking up, and seeing money mentality inside my head. At first, I picked up a job in a printing press in Awka, I worked there for only a few months and I resigned, When people asked me why I resigned I answered that it was not the kind of work and life that I wanted for myself. But part of the truth was that I worked hard working eight hours a day only to be earning a little Eight thousand Nigeria Naira (8000) in a month for my monthly pay cheque as a graduate. It got to a point where I couldn't continue working like an elephant but eating like an ant. Most of the time resigning from a current job when you don't have any alternative for any other source of income is always difficult, too hard but it always requires bold courage. When I resigned from working in the printing press and began to stay at home day after day doing nothing, following with the current state of my joblessness my thoughts of Sleep, waking up, and seeing money reincarnated within my mind as I began to fashion and nurture the thought again and again. It is said what one continuously thinks about that will begin to attract its kind in the physical realm that leading to manifestation.

One day I was taking a walk along Unizik junction in Awka it is an area mainly dominated by university students schooling at Nnamdi Azikiwe University, when I stumble a group of young students sharing flyers, Seeing how fashionable and richly these students dressed I was quicken in my heart and admire their gallant dressing but still keep to my direction. Excuse me one of the students in the group beckoned on me, I stopped and she approached me She first exchanged pleasantries with me handed one of the flyers to me, and asked me one question if I had heard of an online business opportunity that leverages most young people to riches. With that bullet point statement, I was captivated by her question as I relaxed my inner spirit to hear more from her. I gently replied to her that I hadn't heard of any online business like that. I asked if it is Forex trading, and she put up an angelic smile and responded to me, that it is more than Forex trading and more beneficial. Tell me more about your brand of online business I asked her. She went on to explain it as a new brand of business opportunity whereby I will be opportune to leverage on residual profit twenty-four hours every day without buying or selling any product. Before I could ask her any further questions she exchanged phone contact with me and asked me to come for their business summit so every question I had in mind to ask her would be addressed on that day more comprehendible for me, I thanked her and went on my way but I kept pondering on the business idea I heard from her, I was thinking in my head is this kind of another Bitcoin news or other kind of business opportunity? I asked a lot of questions in my mind, I couldn't say no to such a business seminar when I had been proposed to a new business opportunity that smoothened my heart and ear, whereas I am still unemployed, jobless having nothing to do at that time.

On the date of the business summit according to the flyer I put on my best clothes and headed off, getting to the venue of the business seminar ground, which was held in one of the best hotels in Awka, I saw a lot of flashy mighty cars parked I was so marveled in my heart as I was seriously asking rhetorical questions in my mind what kind of business is this that people will come for it with mighty cars like this, I buckle up my mind and went inside the hotel conference room only to behold young students neatly and richly fashioned, the business seminar kick start as the moderator ushers in the main man that pioneer the business name Smart Alozie, the young man was richly dress, fried his hair and speaks fluently and softly. He introduced the name of the online business as E-Business Network (EBN), It is a multi-leveraged online Network Marketing business. The young man pitches this business well package and shows the most proof that is testament and so convincing on how the business has affected lives positively, the traveling trip by the business members that have come up to a certain stage in the business, the free give away luxury cars and a whole lot of other good shreds of evidence, he calls up some students who have really made it big in the business, when most of the students were asked to unveil their account dashboard it was huge thousands of dollars in there. I was marveled becoming more intensely captivated seeing more of the proof and the status of these young students driving luxury cars. I was very interested in this kind of business because it is related to my kind of dream of "Sleep, wake, and see money. It was my first time hearing of such an online business opportunity of making money online and at the same time traveling around the world all sponsored by the company. According to this very kind of business the only requirement to start is the startup capital, and to keep earning in the business is to introduce people who will register under me as down liners and I earn from their commission. I left the business seminar fully motivated to start and earn online just as those young students I saw with certain proofs, but the major hindrance for me to start becomes the startup capital of one hundred and five thousand in Nigeria Naira (105k) and secondly is how to get the down liners that will registered under my account as referrals for me to start earning money, as of then that I quit my job I was really financial incapacitated I barely feed three times a day so raising such money to register was a problem as there was nothing I could do to raise such amount of money, I called most people I know to be my family members and friends but because the business is a something they were not familiar with they didn't show interest in it or even volunteer to help me and raise the registration money, It was only one of my sister living in Lagos that has heard little of such online business opportunity and told me of truth that people are cashing out from the business mainly most young people, I was desperately captivated with seriousness the more when she told me her own share of the story about the business news, the online networking business but the annoying part of the story was that she refused giving me the money as she said to me that this might be a tricky way for scammers to siphoned money from people, I immediately banned her opinion regarding such a business as a scam business after seeing the enough prove with my own very eyes. At a point, I got frustrated for not being able to come up with the startup capital to register with the business just like I once did before during my final year in the higher institution in the year 2014/2015 after hearing of Bitcoin, once again this time I gave up again with the business.

**WISE INVESTOR:**
As a newbie in the financial market never be too quick to embrace what you see or what you hear as a business opportunity, in most cases there are a lot of scam sites, Apps, or money-investing platforms camouflaging everything, posing to be real but they are a wolf in sheep clothing targeting people hard earn money, most of these sites are overrated, hype and promise fool's paradise promises that never exist or only exist temporary, many innocent people has lost their funds all because of quick to embrace a fake business opportunity. In the crypto market scammers will create a temporary token and hype the token during the presale stage but after launching the project the whole thing will crash and become history, or developers of a particular token will cause high traffic (sales) bumping money on the token the price will raise up then innocent investors mostly the new investors will be quick to invest their money on the token after a while the price of the token will be crashing down steadfastly till it reduces to nothing but zero value. This is a common game in the crypto and stock market, All that glitters is not gold, Some tokens and stocks are potential assets while most of them are bump-and-dump projects so never be too quick to embrace too good to be a real project but at the

back end of the project it only nothing but a money liquidating presented business opportunity.


## TRAP OF THE PONZI SCHEME (THE BUSINESS OF COMPULSORY GET TWO PERSONS)

With the frustration of not being able to raise the starting capital to register with EBN Networking Business and start making thousands of dollars as I earlier thought, I gave up searching for who would help me out with the capital and move on with my life the way it is.

Early in 2016, I secured a teaching job at the Nigeria Institute of Commerce which it name was later renamed after the owner of the school name as Nwanno Nwimoh. Then, a friend of mine whose name Greatman introduced to me a website called Coolnaira a multi-leverage marketing website (MLM) I got interested in investing with the site simply because the start-up capital was a minimum of five dollars ($5) although the return benefit is not promising like EBN but I decided to start with Coolnaira. I invested with a little start capital considering the fact that I am not financially buoyant as a school teacher. When I registered I was told to get two people that will get another two persons to register under me before I could start earning. Getting two persons to be under me as my downliners I thought it would be that easy but it wasn't, I practically turned to be a marketer preacher of the website down to the point that it became very annoying to me what sort of business is this of compulsory getting two persons that will equally get another two persons as downliners before I can earn or climb to a new level, though I keep pushing preaching to people and friends of the business opportunity, later I was able to secure two people that registered under me but getting my cash out became a problem, I was later told by the team leader that it no longer two persons as a downliners to climb to next level and get cash out but four persons, hearing the news I became very disappointment about the whole thing but I have done a lot for the website, I thought to myself only my preaching is a testament of my hard work for the site. So I made up my mind mandating that I must receive my cash out. I kept pushing and preaching with more effort to people about the site trying all possible best means to convince them to register with the website and be my downliners, I even to a point opened a WhatsApp group where I added most of my friends to the group but it became more frustrating and annoying surprise watching them existing the group one after the other without giving heed to the business. At last, I decided to use my salary and register myself as the two remaining downliners which I did at month end when I received my paycheck but still getting the cash out from Coolnaira site as my benefit still to no avail, this time it became another new story that I should wait a little while for me to be match among the new people to be paid for next month, I was waiting patiently with the hope to receive my cash out when another news reach to me that the website is under maintenance for site upgrading, how long will it takes I asked my friend Greatman who introduced me to the site and also the regional coordinator soon was the reply he gave me as an answer. About two months after I was still waiting for my cash out when the same guy wrote to me on WhatsApp that the site had finished its upgrading and was ready to launch, hearing that I was very happy to withdraw my earnings but he further added a statement that kept my happy mood on a pause, he said to me that withdraws for all old transactions will not be processed because the site has upgraded it operation changing it initial name from Coolnaira to Electronic Boss (E-Boss) and the investment plan altogether with a new incentive plan has all been upgraded that what I only need do is to top up my old initial investment plan to upgrade to the new investment plan so that I can receive a new incentive cash out. At first, I was not satisfied with the new idea but after remembering my hanging capital in the site and also the promising mouth-watering new incentive I was pushed to reconsider, so from the little savings I made from my salary I took out some money and top up my investment plan, I was asked to bring extra two people to be my downliners this time, I bluntly told my friend that when the site was accepting little capital investment to register I couldn't get people to register under me let alone now the site investment capital has increased, the guy seeing the frustration mix with anger in my eyes he promise to help me look for downliners, I get little hope hearing the statement from him. I was waiting to be matched for payment when I heard the ugly heart weakening news that the site had gone for maintenance again and this time that was the end of it all for they never returned again. All my investment capital was lost in Coolnaira and E-Boss, My eyes were opened but I consoled myself as I thought that was one of the encounters someone would stumble upon the way to success.

In late 2016 few months after my encounter with the Coolnaira and E-Boss site, another trending online business investment site saturating the entire country, the news soon was no longer a rumor to me as I constantly heard people giving testimony upon testimony for quick and easy cash-out, when I enquired about the money site I discovered that the name of the money site was **MMM**.

**MMM** was a Ponzi scheme that then had great dominance in the financial market reason because it posed in disguise to be one of the best investment platforms, both young and old knew of MMM that year, I was still managing my life as a school teacher when the wave of this **MMM** money internet business opportunity was brewing making greater impact in the country that it became most people major business and occupation. Most people I knew as friends and family members were testifying on how they had cashed out several times investing on the platform. At first, I was strongly holding myself back from falling for this kind of business deal again not after my previous experience with **Coolnaira** and **E-boss website,** but the constant news of massive cash out from **MMM** was really alarming and equally overwhelming as people were giving testimonies about the site, the news became a major trend on social media. So one day I decided not to be left out in this online investment opportunity that has blessed and changed so many people's lives overnight, so I decided to try my luck and watch the outcome of my luck I registered with the site and invested some portion of amount as my capital investment. A few days after I invested with **MMM** the thought and the spirit of "Sleep, wake up and see money" again was awakened back in my life as I was dreaming and expecting big cashing out through my investment and working nothing, cashing out without doing nothing. So I pulled out all the money in my bank account and spread my investments not only on the **MMM** Platform but also in other investment platforms, One was called **Twinkas** and the other was called **"Ultimate Cycler"** With each minimum startup capital investment, all the sites were promising thirty percent (30%) return of investment. I invested in these three platforms and relaxed hopefully counting the days for my match-up so that I would get my cash out, but the worst tragic thing happened again as the three sites went into relegation as under site maintenance and that was the end of it all as the sites were later shut down from operation, and that was how a majority of people's money including all my savings was frozen and scam, some people committed suicide because of the shock of losing their huge investment capital, so many were driven to huge financial set back and lifetime debt.

I was devastated because my greed has driven huge losses, causing me to lose all my little savings in the bank, For me life is like a fresh start all over again.

**WISE INVESTOR:**
First, Don't be Lazy: I will clearly state that there are no means to get the money that you wouldn't work for it, Even as an investor you still need to work for your money by doing concrete research on any asset you want to invest your money into, if you lack the knowledge to carry out some concrete research study or too lazy to do some investigation before you invest you can implore the knowledge of someone else to do the forecasting for you. When I invested in Coolnaira and E-boss I was told to get two people who would equally bring two people to be under me as my downliners before I could move to level two and access my cash out, I sought out to look for the two persons that lure me to suddenly became a motivational speaker, a marketer and a preacher of business website, it transforms me to become a leader when I created a WhatsApp group, I was busy talking to people about the site working for the platform, but my initial idea was to just invest in the website and relax and watch money magically flow into my bank account

but it wasn't as I thought, the demand of bring referrals to register under me compel me seriously to work for it. So there is no means to make money that does not require working for it, you must do your own work before your money will work for you in return.

Secondly, As a new investor Avoid high expectations of returns: No genuine investment platform can promise to give you Return Of Investment (ROI) by thirty percent (30%). The maximum percent of returns of investment any genuine investment platform can assure is five to ten percent Anything more than that I sincerely advise you never put your money in. I may not be a financial advisor but with the experience I have gotten I can counsel on investment. So as an investor avoid any one or any investment platform promising you mouth-watering high percent returns of your investment, do your diligent findings more about the investment platform, or rather still don't put in your money.

Thirdly, Avoid greed, As a new investor one very negative factor you need to run away from is greed, take away greed from your mind if you want to survive and succeed in investment. Don't invest all your money, at the highest invest only fifty percent of your total income and leave fifty percent in your account as a backup account, Don't make the huge mistake of investing all or almost all of your income in any investment plan.

Don't borrow to invest: Means don't make the mistake of borrowing money be it from the bank or from a friend to start an investment portfolio, Many investors make the mistake of borrowing money to invest, Have you ever reasoned and thought what if something should happen or if the market should crash what will be the outcome. Don't sell a valuable asset to trade or invest in any investment platform rather you can sell a liability and not an asset. During the reign of **MMM** in my country many sold their asset to invest in **MMM** because of the greed of wanting more, higher money return, many borrowed money to invest, and many invest what they cannot afford to lose.

Don't invest what you cannot afford to lose: very important for every beginner to never invest some amount of money in any portfolio you cannot afford to lose. What many investors will fail or will hide to explain is that investing and trading is like or almost equal to gambling, any amount of money you invest in any portfolio is like sacrificial money you have used to gamble in the market, if you are lucky enough you profit from the market if not lucky you lose your money when the market crash. So as a new investor be cautious not to invest an amount you cannot afford to lose.

In summary, run away very far from anything Ponzi scheme of robbing Peter to pay Paul. Before you invest money in any investment site always verify what is the means of the platform sustainability method or plan, such as how they make their money, what they sell, and what they offer,

## MY FIRST GOLD INVESTMENT IN 2017

After the great loss hit with **MMM, Twinkas,** and **Ultimate Cycler,** the year 2016 Christmas celebration was never funny to most Nigerians including myself.
In the second half of the year 2017 some months after the incident lost of investment funds to the wrong platform, then I quit my teaching job and was serving my one-year mandatory national service in Oyo state Nigeria, again My friend Greatman whom earlier talked to me into Coolnaira and E-boss disclose another investment deal again, this time it is a gold plan mining company. Indeed Greatman is a smooth talker, he knows how to smooth his speech, he showed me proof of his cash withdrawal from the site including his bank alert, and he promised me that this very company is reliable and trustworthy and that he has done his research and confirmed that the company is very authentic, he further told me that this is not MLM (Multi Leverage Marketing) where I will be asked to bring two people as downliners before I could be paid, but this is a gold mining company where I only invest my funds with the company and earns from mining and I will also have the advantage to sell my gold if it appreciate in market value. He got my heart and attention again into this new investment deal when he mentioned to me that I don't have to do anything or bother looking for people refer to the website before earning, that my own part is just to invest my capital with the company and watch my money grow like grass as the gold appreciates in the market value and anytime I feel to stop my investment with the company that the gold mining company will ship my raw gold at my address. After saying this and with the proofs he had shown me I decided to give it a try again this time. I registered with the website and invested some amount of money as I patiently monitored my dashboard after investing with the gold mining company, During the same period he brought up another idea of Agricultural investment, a company that deals in food crops that with some amount of startup investment capital I will be entitled to have monthly free foodstuff. I like the idea of gaining from such an offer because according to him the company disburses food stuff to their investors according to the level of investment with the company, The company's food disbursement plan is very mouth-watering so I also send some amount of money to him to registered me with the Agriculture company; I was still waiting and monitoring my gold account dashboard as weeks turn to a month, one month to months but I see no improvement or changes with the figure showing in dashboard.

One day I could not wait anymore I wrote to Greatman and informed him to sell my gold for I wished not to keep the investment anymore, he said he would market it for me and send my money. I also enquired about my food stuff he told me that the woman in charge of our region who was the regional manager had been hospitalized for a health challenge but whenever she is discharged from the hospital he would talk to her about my supposed accumulated foodstuff. A few weeks later Greatman wrote to me that he had marketed my gold for me, though it sounded good to at least let me receive my capital investment back but when I waited for a credit alert in my bank account I saw nothing, I enquire from him again why haven't I receive any money in my bank account he complains to me that the buyer has accepted to buy the gold but the transaction was not processing but to give him some time for the payment to drop in my account. But up till today date I have not had access to reclaim my gold as at first mentioned, I can't sell the gold and I can't withdraw my funds out. Also for the food company that was how I didn't receive anything from the company, The woman he said to be hospitalized I didn't know if she ever regained from her health challenge or not because I didn't hear anything further concerning my foodstuff.

## NGO EMPOWERMENT

In the year 2018, after I had lost it again with my previous investment with the invisible unknown gold mining company and the food company, I faced my reality squarely by believing that I had been scammed again and again by some wrong guys at the other side who has set a bait for people like us to fall in. After the incident, I decided to finally lose contact and connection with this very gentleman called Greatman because he always introduce me to dangerous systems that crippled my hard earn money, though he didn't force me to it rather it was the choice I made by releasing my fund to these wrong guys behind the mask. But this time I was really out of money I was faced with dragging my heavy baggage of hardship, at that present time I was face with menial jobs, I was only surviving with menial jobs I could find in the street, such as container loading and offloading, working as a laborer in building sites, I tried very hard to secure a decent job with my certificate but to no avail, I do not need to give up rather I settle on the common jobs I could find in the street and that was my only way of survival as of then. When life is really cruel to a man he will definitely be seeking for a quick alternative to avail himself of such hardship that was in my own case, I was too eager to resort to possible means of availing myself of the present hardship and enjoying a better life. I was seriously doing wide research about work online and any other resemblance of what can transform my life positively. During the year 2018, a new update came up then it was a new format of some NGOs giving grants to people with good business ideas, also That year the new trend of the World Bank giving out huge amounts of money as grants to most countries to support their youths, this trend automatically becomes a business opportunity in the country as many NGO's are claiming to be among the agent to disburse the money world bank promise to disburse, though definitely there will always be some set of people to testify to have receive funds from most of these masked NGO's agent, as many agents calming to be the right agent while some beneficiaries testifying to have receive funds from them. In my own case looking for survival and anxiously looking for free money to help my life I developed a quick interest to be attracted to these guys' bait, as most of the NGO agents are selling forms for thousands of Naira, many people like me that are eager to receive this money are paying for the forms. With the opportunity to have a share of the free money big, I was engulfed with more greed, selfish-intelligent interest, and wanted by all possible means to get this free money as a grant to escape from my hand-to-mouth life condition I decided to spread my hard earn money I made from my menial jobs by buying these forms from different NGO agents just should in case if my baits fail in one it shouldn't fail in all, I was throwing bait to catch a big fish but never knew that I was instead the big fish baited by these men in the mask to be catch, such is the irony of life. A few months after submitting the forms I purchased from different agents I was expecting to receive money in my bank account because in the form there was a space to fill in bank details to receive the disbursement funds, Then was the year 2018 but from that date up till now I am still waiting hopelessly for this money to drop into my account but I see nothing.

**WISE INVESTOR:**
There is only one simple piece of advice in this passenger story, and It is never **"Try not to take a big risk trying to recover what you have lost before at any cost".** This is a very important statement for every investor, crypto, or stock trader, It will be always too risky in trading and investment chasing countless shadows of your past lost in the market and so therefore desire to bury all your future funds into the present market it is too way risky. This is a very big mistake I made in my foolish way of trying to recover my past loss in the financial market but I instead lost more of my funds. I fail to be more calculative and more details with the people I entrust my money with all because I want a means of recovery. So as a new investor desist from this virus of lost funds recovery in the financial market by all means. It is too risky trying to recover the already lost in the market without being guided properly.

# 2019 MY JOURNEY TO CRYPTOPCURRUNCY

Five years after I heard about Bitcoin from a friend Kinsley during my final year in college, the year 2019 was my first time ever to attempt investing in Bitcoin but by this time the price of Bitcoin had already surged up to a greater value compared to it formal price at first time I heard of it in the 2014. It is quite true that I tried all possible means in the year 2014 to secure a little portion of Bitcoin after hearing it for the first time from a friend whose name is Kinsley but I would also say that my best wasn't good enough, I didn't try harder purchasing the token because I gave up along the line when I did my little research on how to buy Bitcoin after I graduated from college. Later in the year 2019, I was able to secure a small portion of Bitcoin using the Luno Crypto exchange App, then the current price of One Bitcoin was trading at ten thousand Dollars ($10,000) but closed its price that year at seven thousand two hundred dollars ($7200) I started my journey of cryptocurrencies with just some little amount of money, I invested in Bitcoin some few dollars bucks, again I added Litecoin to my portfolio as of then one Litecoin was trading at fifty-eight dollars ($58) I purchased one litecoin because I was able to afford it then, I also added Etherum and Bitcoin Cash (BCH). I just invested some amount of dollars on each of the coins and monitored the price movement, The truth was that I never knew anything about the market chart all I knew then was to monitor the price chart and know when my money increased in value or reduced in value. Every now and then I will always be on Luno App monitoring my investment, I always wish the price to keep increasing in value, everything began to seem real to me when I started seeing my investment capital increasing in figures, deep inside me I felt yes that this is the right investment I had made so far, though at times I saw my investments depreciate in figures when the market trend drops but within me, I still always have the confident that Market will appreciate back, I began seriously adding more funds on each of my portfolios. If you ask me I will confidently say that my investment in Crypto currency is the only legit and best investment so far for me ever since 2016 I started investing in the wrong sites.

## WISE INVESTOR:

Ever since the introduction of Bitcoin in the year 2009 Crypto currency has become a bigger project that has come to stay, It might not have the capacity to replace fiat entirely globally due to its unfamiliar adaption it will take time to be fully accepted around the world as a purchasing power digital currency but I will like to say that it has become a strong competitive major digitalize currency to compete with fiat in the market, the only reason that can slow down the adaption of crypto currencies around the globe in most countries is government policy. Most countries are kicking against the new currencies while in some countries digital currency as crypto has been accepted to trade in the market as a means of accepting payments. So the lesson of the story is to invest in crypto, Don't be afraid of what might happen tomorrow and be left out in this opportunity of investing in crypto now, because even till tomorrow crypto will still be accepted. Buy some good tokens now and invest, It is not a must for you to buy Bitcoin because with the way high price the token is trading on currently but you can buy other crypto projects the price is much more affordable but has much potential, trade crypto if you have knowledge of the market. Don't keep doubting the project. But before going into the crypto space please be sure you have at least basic knowledge of fundamental analysis and if you want to go into day trading make sure you have a combination of fundamental and technical analysis. Don't just jump into the market blindly and never be greedy with the market when putting in your money. Remember to always invest what you can afford and what you can bear to lose should in case the market go against your expectation.

## MY FALL WITH INTERNET SCAM

The late year 2019 I became a YouTube regular site visitor, The truth is there are many things I never knew about but during my cause of frequenting YouTube site, I gained a lot of self-knowledge and personal development. I play on different video categories such as Self-help, Public speaking, and entertainment but above all, I played mostly on wealth and financial education. I played on financial development, and how to make money online either with little or no capital start-up. I subscribed to so many YouTube channels that make videos on how to make money online doing little tasks on websites that are willing to pay for it but there is one Youtuber whom I became addicted to his video content on how to make money online, His YouTube channel name is Wesley Virgin. I was an addicted fan of Wesley Virgin, I followed up on all the videos he dropped on his channel and never missed any because I turned on his channel notification button so that any time he dropped a new content I would be notified. I embrace the young man channel and always follow up on every of his information on how to make money online with no doubt.

One day after watching one of his usual captivating amazing video content I came on the comment section to express my profound appreciation of interest in the wonderful information he packed up for us his fans in the very video, in the comment section I stumbled upon a comment drop by Wesley Virgin the comment read "I am willing to connect my fans to Mr. Jack who is an expert Forex Trader who has to help me make a huge profit over the week, for interested fans WhatsApp him on this WhatsApp number and tell him I refer you to him because I get referral commission" And under this very comment many testifiers comments were thanking him for introducing Mr. Jack to them and how they have made so much profit trading with him. Because of my acute love and belief in Wesley Virgin, I trusted his comment I copied the US foreign WhatsApp number with a dial code +1, I chatted with the number and told him that I am a fan of Wesley Virgin and he referred us his fans to him for trading assistance. Mr. Jack told me his trading terms and conditions that people who invested with him get their trading profit on the weekend after five trading days through Cryptocurrency Usdt Coin and the minimum capital he trades with is five hundred dollars ($500) to ten thousand dollars and above. For the respect and trust I have for Wesley Virgin believing the recommendation came from him I accepted Mr. Jack term and decided to start with five hundred dollars trading package because that was the amount I could easily afford, he sent me his Usdt wallet address where I transferred five hundred dollars, after depositing the five hundred dollars into the Usdt wallet address he provided I was anxiously counting down the five trading days for my trading profit and capital to be return onto me so that I could receive my money and reinvest with it, at the end date that ellipse the five trading days I chatted Mr. Jack but that was the end because he never replied my message the next thing I noticed was that I was blocked out from the WhatsApp contact list that was when I knew that I had been scam I bitterly bear the lost of five hundred dollars because there is nobody I could complain to, I went to one of Wesley Virgin video content and wrote out my complaint and my experience with Mr. Jack he recommended to us as a trusted expert trader but I never got any reply for my complaint. I bitterly bear my loss and learned an additional bitter lesson from the experience.

## WISE INVESTOR:

In reality, I failed to know that the comment I saw in one of Wesley Virgin's videos was not truly a comment from the real Wesley Virgin, but a comment made by an internet fraudster who impersonated everything about him. What these scammers do is impersonate people's accounts and operate as the supposed real person, they will also open multiple YouTube accounts with different email accounts using different fake pictures and user names and commenting on the same comment as though people replied to comments as if it were different people reacting on the comment post. But in a real sense, it is one scammer sitting somewhere else manipulating the whole accounts and any newbie who did not know about this format will weakly fall into their trap. The comment format is always in this systematic order, first, the scammer will drop a comment with one social account (either on Facebook or YouTube account whichever site they are operating from) on how an expert trader helps him in trading Forex and make a huge profit and the same scammer will create testimonial traffic of comments on the first comment as though different people were attesting to his comment to be true but the reality is that it one person commenting with multiple accounts in order to make it look real and engaging, he will drop a WhatsApp number or telegram link, It is through the WhatsApp number or telegram channel link they will execute their malicious mission. Some of these scammers create fake websites to convince and deceive their prey more into believing in their work so the innocent client will release funds to them without having a strong double mind. There easily targeted YouTube video content where they exploit their deceiving plots are mainly videos on finances, such as Forex trading videos, Make Money online videos, Crypto Trading and investment videos, and Financial or business coach, these are the categories of videos where you can easily finds these fraudsters.

Telegram is the citing base of many internet fraudsters indulging in fake trading and investment formats, they clone many real financial brokers in Telegram using their Telegram business name to create a fake Telegram channel and scam people, some of them create a website that looks like the real financial broker's website and direct their client to the website to prove their work like being authentic. Their format of scam pattern is always as follows:

Provide free trading signals and Financial news which they do in copy and paste format, they copy whatever thing they are pasting in their channel from the original financial broker's telegram channel or their fellow scammer's telegram channels. They offer fake trading signal subscription packages Weekly, Monthly, and Yearly starting from fifty dollars to two hundred dollars. They offer fake trading investment packages starting from two hundred or five hundred dollars to ten thousand dollars and above with huge return profit in five or three trading days. They filled up their telegram channel with inorganic members buying telegram members online, that is why if you are a telegram user sometimes you find yourself in an unknown channel you did not subscribe to, if you accidentally see yourself in such channel by mistake you didn't subscribe to, I advise you quickly opt-out from such channel and help Telegram by reporting such account so that they will take the appropriate action on such fake impersonating account.

These internet fraudsters mainly operate on three dimensions in which they get their targeted client that fall into their trap which they are:

Dating scam: This format of scam that the perpetrators engage their client through online dating, they impersonate people's social media profiles or hack people's profile accounts to carry out their deeds, this category of scammers specializes in hunting online lovers freaks. So beware of the person you are chatting with as an online lover. Their marketplace to hurt clients is mainly dating Apps.

Investment Scam: This category of scammers are those earlier discussed, they offer to help you build your finance by asking you to invest or trade with them either in Crypto, Forex, or in any property they fake to sell forging fake digital document, or passport using the right tools like Canva and Photoshop to create fake digital documents.

Hackers: This is the professional stage of internet scammers, this category of scammers bomb their clients through back doors, they first create phishing bait for their prey either through email or through social text message that is clickable once you click on the message it lands you on a malicious site, they hack into public and private Wi-Fi mostly public Wi-Fi, that is why you should be careful when connecting to public free Wi-Fi, in the bus station, public park, schools, and restaurants, they can hack into people bank credit card, Crypto wallet, website, and anything hackable to execute malicious act.

Lastly, it is very advisable that living in this internet age you should know basic about Cyber security to quickly protect and defend from cyber intruders such as scammers; it helps you to protect your data and prevent financial loss.

You protect yourself from these internet wolves by first having the knowledge of how they operate then you can easily defend yourself when you come in contact with them and how to protect yourself from their phishing tactics to push them off not getting into your account. It is very important you know how they operate and that is why this very book is one of the essential books you should have in your book self.

## 2020 MY JOURNEY TO FOREX TRADING

During the time of the world pandemic crisis, the whole world seemed to stand still due to nothing was much happening because of the virus and the lockdown problem, The company where I worked was facing the challenge of the lockdown order so I was sitting at home doing nothing I was eager to sort for another alternative of income flow but I couldn't think out anything so reasonable, I resort my search online on YouTube I came across so many videos about Forex trading and how people are cashing out from it, for me it was wow seeing the reality on how this Forex is turning people into mega rich, among all the videos I stumbled on YouTube no one seems to be talking about the risk involve in this trade. Nevertheless, Forex trading is what I heard about years ago but I never called it anything because for me I keep wondering what sort of trade is buying currency against currency online, but now we are in lockdown I need to seek an alternative way to be making money online. After seeing those videos I was captivated with people mighty testimonies I saw online and I decided to gave it try, first I downloaded some of the trading app, the first trading app I downloaded to try out this trade was Olymp trading App. I funded my account and traded but I fail woefully, I practice extensively with the virtual fund in the demo account I will succeed but when I funded my live account again and trade I will lose all my funds, I funded my account with Olymp trading App five times but I fail woefully in the five times attempt, I advised myself to stop, later I decided to try trade with other Forex trading app so to ascertain what I am not doing right or if it is the trading App Olymp is to be blame for my trading failure, so I downloaded OctaFx trading App but same experience I got in Olymp trading app is replaying again as I was practicing with the demo account, I was gaining in the demo account and I thought that it will be that easy I quickly fund my live account in my one, two trade I opened I was liquated easily, I was pain so much watching my money burn to flame, I go back and practice more with the demo trading when I thought that I have learnt some technical techniques in the App again I funded my live account but still I was liquated easily, I fund again, at this time I profited some dollars and I was very happy as I cast more lot before I knew what was happening again I was liquated, I made up my mind to stop funding my live account because at the quest of trying to make money I was seriously losing more money that will help me to sustain till the end of the pandemic but on a second thought I stubbornly wanted to recover my money that I have lost In the process, I funded again I was liquated, later I realize that there is an option in the trading App called copy trading, meaning that I can simply copy a trader or invest my fund with a professional trader to trade for me, I decided to go for the option, first I funded my account again and copy a first trader but it wasn't successful, I fund again and this time choose another trader again it was not successful, I did that for five different traders but all fail, at this time I didn't need anyone to advise me to stop wasting my money, I didn't allow my stubbornness to ruin me out entirely I quitted funding further by all means, I was trying to get money but I was instead speedily loosing the little money I ready have to an unknown people at the other side of the trading App. I quit trading Forex even as I continue seeing serials of testaments of people's success stories on Forex online I blindly neglect and overlook it all, experience is the best teacher they said.

## WISE INVESTOR:
Trading Forex requires deep knowledge of trading tactics, trading Forex is not as easy as many will think it is, it requires commitment, focus, patience, and above all knowledge of trading and the market you want to enter, knowing the time to enter the market and time to exit the market, knowing most of the technical analysis of trading, reading the trends lines and following the financial news, I made so much mistake on my part hoping that trading is just be built on guessing work trial by error, and working with the little knowledge I learned on YouTube without having anyone to have coached me enough with the knowledge I needed to know about the financial market.

Secondly, never follow the deceiving trait of a demo account in most Trading Apps, Yes, I call the demo account deceitful because when trading on demon account you don't trade with emotion or with fear of losing your money, you trade with careless mind, unserious mindset, you trade with greed and not with caution of losing your real money, so having this kind of mindset trading the Forex market will never make you understand the market, the chart pattern or called market movement. But when you are trading with real money you will be more caution with yourself of not been greed to cast a single trade with a huge amount of money, you will know how to set your risk management; you will learn to know chart pattern or candle pattern that works. And also remember that technical analysis is limited financial news, and Government Policy that chart pattern can not detect.

Lastly, some of these Forex Trading Apps are not to be trusted, they are not legit, some are scams, some are deceitful, some are programmed in a way to liquidate people's funds once you switch to a live trading account, and they are a wolf in sheep clothing. In my research, I discovered that some of the trading Apps have gone into extinction and are no longer operating while the real trading Apps are still operating to date.


**MY FAIL INVESTMENT WITH FOREX TRADING COMPANY**

In the year 2020 after the ease of three months lockdown in Nigeria, life began to come back to normal gradually. We were asked to resume work back in the office but at this time I did not have much in my savings account because I had been spending from my savings account all through the lockdown period and nothing was coming in plus my huge losses trying to trade on Forex. In the middle of the year 2020 few month after the ease of lock down another information reaches to me of a particular firm that is into Forex trading, they publicly trade Forex for people that invest with them and also conduct trading coaching, the name of the trading firm was MBA Forex trading which the chairman of the firm name is Maxwell Odum. one day I made my way to their office location in Enugu state where I live to make enquire on how they operate, I was told that the minimum investment trading capital to invest with them is one thousand dollars (($1000) which was equivalent of four hundred thousand Nigeria Naira then in black market exchange rate, and the return of investment is fifty percent return of investment (ROI) I was captivated by the huge promising return of investment but what I don't really have at that moment was the complete investment capital, the total money I was having in my bank savings account was not up to the total amount but I was drawn in lost with the promising percentage of the (ROI) return of investment, I left the office and started thinking on how to make up with the amount, I even thought of going to my bank to borrow some amount of fund to invest with the company, so one day I set out to my bank reaching there I told them I need a loan for some account of money but to my ultimate surprise my bank turn me down of granting me the loan, I felt dejected in my heart of why will my own bank will deny me of access to obtain a loan with them I left the bank premises feeling disappointed but I didn't not give up the idea of investing with the company what I did was to give myself some time to receive some of my monthly salary after the ease of the lock down. I received three months of my salary added it up with some money in my savings account and marched straight to MBA Forex office with the capital investment, Getting to the office I was feeling big within me that soon I would have a second authentic stream of income apart from my monthly salary. I registered with the company accepted their term of service and deposited my whole savings with them went home with gladness in my heart, one upper month my church Pastor introduced to me another investing site and assured me of the site's authenticity with a series of testimonies of how people are cashing out from the site, me using the influence that he is my Pastor and believing he wouldn't lie to me rather he always wants the best for me and any other of his church members, though the capital investment is not that much compare to MBA Forex trading, so I decided to try out the site and I invested some amount of money with the site as I was really feeling excited hoping that I has gotten multiple source of income even when the income has not start coming in yet. In MBA Forex according to their terms of operation, I am supposed to start receiving cash out of my return on investment the next month after opening a new account. Reaching the actual month after I had impatiently waited to start receiving my profit into my bank account but at the end of it second month I received nothing in my bank account, then I became worried I planned to visit their office when I got to their office of operation and made my complain they gave me some reasons of excuses why my money has been delayed, after the end of third months, it was the end of the fourth month yet I received nothing when I visited their office I found no one in the office, the office was closed, I further inquiry about the company it happens to be that the company has shut down it operation closing down all their branch offices in the country and folding up with millions of people's money including my own money, hearing the news it was like a dream of hell to me all my savings is what I used to open an account with the company, I took the little remaining strength in me and walk back home, Same year during December period the site my church Pastor introduces to me was closed down. That was how I was scammed the whole of my entire savings in my account, but thanks to the Almighty creator that I did not use the bank loan to open an account If not I would have been pained that I was scammed and also in agony on how to pay back the bank loan with an additional interest.

**WISE INVESTOR:**
First, after my ugly incident with MBA Forex I learned a bitter lesson that no real investment company can promise a huge mouth-watering return of investment to clients to the average of fifty percent return of interest (ROI), I learned that any investment company promising to give fifty percent of return of investment to their clients should be much looked in to, be questioned and to be avoided. The highest a legit investment company can promise their clients should not be more than five to ten percent return of investment, fifteen to twenty percent return of investment should also be looked into, but the probability I am rating at any investment company promising a return of investment ranging from fifteen to twenty percent ROI should be thirty to forty percent probability of surviving the company or folding up the company, but any investment company promising fifty percent return of investment should be avoided entirely because there is nothing like sustainability in the company, they will definitely fold up one day and scamp with people's money. I will never advise anyone to entrust their money to any financial investment company with the promise of a fifty percent return on investment.

Another thing important to do is to deeply research about a company before leasing your money out, Know their services, know what they offering, selling, or buying If it is a trading and investment company try know their deep sustainability, know how long they have been existing and how long they have been functioning based on their service, know how they make a profit that can help keep the company running, let it not be that they are doing rob Peter to pay Paul make your research very diligently about the company before trusting out your money.

Lastly, I will never recommend borrowing funds from family, or friends, or using a bank loan to make an investment, it is very too risky, Investing is just like gambling, two things are always involved either you benefit from the investment or you lose, but let it be that you are using your own money and amount you can afford to lose whenever making an investment. And always invest with the money you see as spare money and not with your entire savings, Never invest all of your savings in a particular project or stock, always think of a backup plan in case your investment backfires you will have what to fall back to.

## 2020 THE DECLINE OF CRYPTOCURRENCY IN NIGERIA

Everything was going on smoothly with crypto trading and investment in Nigeria of buying and selling crypto directly from Nigeria banks not until in the year 2020 the Nigeria government under the administration of President Muhammadu Buhari announced the stop of Crypto transactions with Nigeria banks, this negative news cause great crypto havoc in Nigeria as many Crypto holders and traders, people like me became afraid thinking that this new Nigeria policy on Crypto might cause great lost of investment, so, many Nigerians out of fear began selling off their tokens, I was not left out in this category of people, with the fears that I have lost so much in investment starting in the year 2016, I don't want history to repeat itself, so now that I still have the opportunity I thought it right to sold out all my crypto investments. A few months after that I sold out all my tokens in my investment wallet Crypto currency experienced a huge turnaround of Bull Run in the market as the price began to soar high each week, I was watching the tokens price perform well but I couldn't buy any Crypto anymore because of the new Nigeria policy against Crypto transaction from the bank. Though I don't have any funds in my investment wallet but I keep monitoring the market and any time I see the tokens increase in price I weep in my heart, Though no outflow of eyes from my eyes but I weep in my heart because this would have been my greatest opportunity to really make it big in crypto investment. The Bull Run continued till in the year 2021, when Bitcoin price reached its all-time high in price value of sixty-five thousand dollars ($65,000) per token, During this period every other coin reached its all-time high in higher price value. Nigeria's policy makes me lose out big in the market Bull Run for I only watch the price goes up but never partake of it.

**WISE INVESTOR:**
In this very passage of this story, I allowed my emotions to play a huge role in my investment. Fear is a fast killer of things most especially in the financial market. In trading and investment don't bring in your fears, don't allow your emotions to play a major role, and take away emotion if you want to succeed in the financial market. If you bring in emotion it will cripple your mentality to calculate well, that is why most times people feel comfortable trading the market with a trading Bot that doesn't have any emotion when trading, it only executes the command of buying when necessary and selling when necessary, but when compared to human trading judgment emotion is always applicable, As a trader and an investor keep away emotion from your business.

What I really fail to understand simply because I allow my emotions to cripple me was that Crypto currency is not just an invention for a particular country or some particular countries rather crypto is a new digital currency that was developed with the intention of global acceptance and not just limited to any particular legion, so if the policy issued out about crypto was announced in Nigeria it doesn't mean it changes the crypto market making the project to go into extinction or that Nigeria policy against crypto will stop other countries from trading Crypto. But because of fear allowing my emotions to ride over me, I decided to sell off every one of my tokens making me miss out greatly during the year 2021 Crypto Bull run. Don't trade and invest clouded with your human emotions otherwise, you will fail in the financial market.

### 2021 MY ENCOUNTER WITH SHIT COINS

At the end of the year 2021, many crypto exchange Apps found a way to boycott Nigeria's policy of refusing
bank transaction with the crypto exchange App, Luno exchange App introduced a third-party payment site to enable their Nigerian customers to trade Crypto with their App, When I learned about the new Luno development I couldn't wait to dive into the market again because to me I was bitter enough that I have miss out much enough in the bull run, so with the anger in my mind that I really lost out much enough in the market Bull run I quickly fund my trading wallet with almost all my savings so that I can quickly buy some tokens and benefit from the ongoing Bull run, I bought all the tokens I wanted to invested into in their all time high prices expecting that was how the market works that the price will continuously keep going up but to my ultimate surprise after purchasing the tokens at their all time high prices the market trend retrace it trends against my expectation as the market gradually began to go down causing a huge depreciation in my investment I was

still expecting and believing that the market will revise and perform well but it never did rather the market keeps going downtrends seeking new lower low almost every week, that was how I lost greatly in my crypto investment. But still, I didn't angrily sell off the tokens I watched it seeking new low almost every week but I left the investment like that.

Later that same year a friend of mine introduce me to shit coins or Alternative coins popularly abbreviated as Alto coins or Hot coins in Crypto terms, he further told me a story of how he became an overnight multi-millionaire through investing in shit coins, he also told me the story of a token called Shiba Inu which was created on 2020 but soars in price in the year 2021 which makes many of it earlier investors multi-millionaires in dollars and some profit in thousands of dollars, he further explained to me that investing in Bitcoin or other tokens that have gone high in the price can never make me rich if I don't have enough capital to invest because the price of Bitcoin per bit has overgrown my financial capability which is true because there is no way I could have be able to afford the price of one Bitcoin considering the level of my financial status then. He advised me to channel my investment on newly developed tokens that just ends their presale, seeing the testament from this friend and also the level of his financial transformation all I see is evidence of the truth of what he advised, this very guy was lucky enough to be an earlier investor of some shit coins that appreciate mightily in the market and vomit excess return of investment, I literally watched this very guy start his hotel building project with the aid of his investment in shit coin. I gave heed to his advice as I quickly swift into coingecko website and started searching out some shit coins to buy without having any knowledge about shit coins. Eventually I was able to buy some shit coins as I could, then I have extended using other Crypto exchange Apps such as Metamask, Binance, Coinbase, and Trust wallet, so I traded most of these shit coins on Trust wallet and on Metamask, but the worst happens, I invested two hundred dollars ($200) each on shit coin project accumulating about twelve different shits coins making it a total of two thousand four hundred dollars ($2400) I staked in shit coins, I staked my investment like that hoping that out of all the scattered investments that one or more will give me a good turn up profit of 10x and above, but unfortunately for me as I watched all the twelve shit coins depreciated in price rapidly till my investment capital runs into zeros, and till date never do they appreciate anymore.

**WISE INVESTOR;**
First I will say to use knowledge and follow the market whenever you want to trade in the financial market and do not be too quick to rush into the market and stake at a particular market point of entry level but before you stake at market entry

make sure you have studied the trend analysis very well and know the price movement, and know when to exit the market when you profit or when the market is turning against you. There is always a system of trading which you must learn the system first before you trade on the financial market, if not you will be on the verge of quick loss or total liquidation of your funds. if you want to trade in the financial market and you lack the technical knowledge of the market I will advise you to use the brain of someone else who knows the trading tactics to serve as a guidance or assistant person, Don't first do it yourself if you don't know trading techniques.

The Ponzi scheme mode of operation is now been operated in the crypto space, the era of **MMM** kind of Ponzi mode of operation has been exposed and people can easily point out such kind of investment scheme as a scam. The illegal business is now trending in the Crypto space but it takes only a few people to understand this Ponzi scheme in the Crypto space. The majority of Crypto developers are in the business of Ponzi operation, every day about thousands of tokens are developed, and many are publicly launched and listed on various Crypto exchange sites, but not all of these thousands of tokens developed every day have future potential, The majority of the tokens are all bump and dump project. So before you start investing in Alto coins make sure you are satisfied with the token white paper but even as that white paper is not a guarantee that a token has a future potential.

The initial plan of developing a crypto currency is for the good of decentralizing the financial space so that centralized entities (i.e. banks) will have control of people's transactions. This very intention was what birthed Crypto currency. The Man who earlier wrote the white paper on Bitcoin the first crypto coin mainly specifies it as a means to give people a legitimate peer-to-peer electronic cash system that wouldn't rely on bank authority. But in recent times most men in the mask have high jack the original intention of Satoshi Nakamoto the brain behind the creation of Bitcoin set the crypto space as a gambling space of buying and holding and day trading and no longer the original intent as primarily developed as new digital electronic cash exchange of goods and services. It is said that every good thing must have men in the mask to adulterate it for the purpose of their greed and self-benefit. These men in the masks are now everywhere in the Crypto space called Whales, These Whales powerfully influence the market for their own self-gain and for other reasons, they pump in money in some of these newly developed tokens that cause the price of the token to shoot up that newbies in the crypto market will believe that the very particular token is performing well in the market they will rush in and invest their money in the project when the Whales has seen the rush in of the average investors in that particular project (token) and knowing that their profit investment in the token has triple 10x they will pull out their money from the token by selling their shares in the project causing the token to makes a drastically revise to create a downtrend and crash many people money, they the Whales has gain massively from the token by playing peoples mind and benefiting from their money. it is also like that in the stock market and not only in the Crypto space, The same people who earlier caused this system of biased trading in the stock market before the development of the Crypto space are the same brain behind that has inflicted this same system of bias trading of pump and dump project system of trading in Crypto space.

Another set of Men in the mask in the Crypto space use the tactic to develop a fake temporary project (token) launch it in the market get it hyped by paying bloggers to talk good of the project, pump the project with their money, and lure innocent people to invest their money in the project during the presale, once they have gotten to how much money that is satisfying for them they will pull out their money by selling their shares allow the project to crash and that all for the project for it will never rise again. These two different tactics Men in the mask or people on the other side are using their money to trap other people's money in their pockets using their tactics system to cash out big in the market by playing on the majority of innocent investors who don't know the trick in the financial market. That is why I will always say that trading and investing in the financial market is like the same thing as gambling, If coming into the financial market you need to come in with your head meaning come in with your common sense and not blindfolding eyes coupled with greed, for if you use an empty brain with a more blindfold eye and enter the financial market without proper guidance or knowledge of how the financial market works coupled with a greedy heart to quick cash out big the end will always be financially disastrous. In the space of anything that has to deal with money, it is always like gambling because even in sports, the sports organizers do sell out their game at times and leave the innocent gamblers suffering for it causing massive loss of bets. But in the world of gambling, there must be a minority that will be lucky to benefit from it while the majority will suffer for the cause, That is the same in the financial market, those that benefit and those that lose. So the summary of the advice is always use your head and don't be quick to be greedy.

## MY ENCOUNTER WITH A CRYPTO DAY TRADER

The same year I met a friend whose name is Emmanuel, It happened that I met this very guy in church, so after the Sunday service we were holding a believers circle, and in the group that I belong to we were asked to introduce ourselves and what we do for a living, in the group, a young man introduces himself as Emmanuel and said he is a crypto trader and a coach. Before that moment, I had always heard of how successful people doing crypto day trading and how they are making a huge profit from it for those who know how to trade, I have always developed an interest in learning day trading and not just limited to buying and holding waiting for a long time till the market appreciate before I make a profit, for me I just want to learn Crypto trading and investing so that I could take it as a full-time business. So back and down to the storyline, after the believers circle meeting I walked up to this guy called Emmanuel, I sincerely told him my ultimate interest in learning crypto day trading, and at that instant, we exchanged phone contact and promised to keep in touch, later on, we book a for a meeting at a spot right there Emmanuel explained to me all his term of coaching and told me many stories about his success and failure in trading but according to him his success outweigh his failure. Down to the line of billing, he billed me some amount of money for the training course, because of my eagerness to learn the trade I agreed to pay the price, and we planned on time and weekdays for the training session, though the training commerce as he was first teaching me the basic of how to buy coins from my Binance spot wallet, but to me the basic teachings is not really what I wanted because I already knew the aspect of fundamental analysis in buying and selling Crypto in the exchange App, that level of teaching is what I already taught myself with the little I learned from YouTube, at most times Emmanuel will never be available to teach me and he will always make excuses and will spices everything up with am sorry. Weeks turned months I still have not learned anything from him, I still not started practicing day trading, and each time I reminded him that it was because of my eagerness to learn Crypto day trading that was why I paid him to teach me but he still not did any good to improve his lessons. At that same period I decided to invest into a token called Wakanda inu and Shiba Inu, I have tried to buy the token myself on Binance but Wakanda inu token is not listed on Binance but the token was listed in a trading App called Rouqq, and again I can't buy from Rouqq because I earlier had an account with the App but lost the login details and I can't open a new account, Emmanuel suggested that he will help me buy the token from his own app and send it to my Trust wallet, so I gave him the money to buy the two tokens for me Wakanda inu and Shiba Inu, but the guy later ended up buying only Shiba Inu tokens for me and promises to buy Wakanda Inu later which I accepted what he said believing the fact that he had already delivered the Shiba inu tokens remaining the Wakanda inu, though after some weeks past he never buy the wakanda Inu as he gives the excuse that Wakanda inu token has deeply deprecated enough in the market and he will recommend I should invest my money into another token, I accepted as he had advised but I waited him to refund my money but he did not, later he further explain that he will research another profiting token with potentials he will recommend for me and buys it with the money earlier meant for Wakanda inu, In other to still maintain tranquility I accepted his decision but waited for the new token he promised to research on and buy but to no avail still. One day Emmanuel came up to me with a new proposal that he was working on creating his own brand of token he called NAB finance which has taken most of his time and caused his unavailability to take me in class, at this point I was already giving up on him seeing that he is not what I thought he is, knowing that he always has an excuse to give in every of his unpleasing act, he has not really taught me the crypto trading I paid him and secondly he was yet to research out the new token he said he will look out for and buy for me in replacement of my Wakanda inu I paid him earlier and yet he doesn't want to refund the money. One particular month he texted me and joyfully told me that he had concluded his project in creating his token and was about to go on presale, he said to me I should be one of his early investors by purchasing the token before the public presale will start, he said the minimum buying price will be one thousand dollars ($1000) I am never interested in this development because he has not really proved to me the right person I earlier thought of him, I told him I don't have up to that amount to invest so therefore, I couldn't be partakers to be among the first investors, he later bring it down by smoothing his talk that because he has really wasted my time by not teaching me what I paid him for and moreover he is still owing my investment capital for the Wakanda inu I should pay him just about two hundred dollars ($200) instead one thousand dollars ($1000) as a minimum investment for hundred thousand NAB Finance tokens. After much thought in my head, I decided to make up my mind and try him out for the last time and also prevent him from reaching me further, so I sent him the money through Usdt using my Binance exchange App, he sent the tokens hundred thousand NAB finance on my Trust wallet but just as if my guess was correct about him that was all, for the token never come to exist in the public market, the project dies with its dreams,. The tutorial I paid him he never taught me, the money I gave him to buy Wakanda inu for me he pocked the money, and the two hundred dollars I sent to him for the NAB finance token he dies the money.

**WISE INVESTOR:**
The lesson to learn here from the passenger of this story is my weakness of quick to trust, my mistake of trusting someone I knew not before with money simply because I met him in the church. Never should you entrust anyone be it a friend, family member, or a fellow religion member when it comes to things that have to deal with money without a proper agreement written on paper and with the witness of a third party involve from both sides or one side. Don't be too quick be foolish to trust someone or do business with a person without getting to know the person's

integrity all around mostly in the area of finance because when it comes to matters of money it is always hard to find genuine repentance, love or trust from people not minding how dear the person is to you, don't believe because you meet the person in a religious believers circle or because he is a family person or a family friend and entrust your money on the fellow without proper agreement, don't try that because it is too dangerous. I have seen so many people who have been dealt with bitterly by their loved ones when it comes to the matter of handling money. Someone might be too good in every other thing or look so innocent but not when it comes to the area of money that once a good person can instantly change to bad, the true color is always out because the power of money has beclouded the person guilt. The spirit of money always drives so many to become sudden betrayals.

## 2022 THE MEGA SCAM

In the year 2022 June 25th I relocated from my home country Nigeria to Sweden, I was just new in the country as an immigrant I was faced with many life challenges, I was presented with menial jobs in the country which was against my choice I detest those kind of job so much that I resorted in seeking for another options in order to augment my life to enable me reach the stage I want In life. I remembered about crypto day trading but on second thought I felt it to be unwise to trade with the available funds in my Binance spot wallet, then I had a total amount of three thousand eight hundred dollars ($3,800) in my Binance wallet. I was afraid to trade by myself because I had heard of the risk involved in future trading and never wanted to blow up my investment but after much struggling with fears I summoned up the courage to engage with future trading believing that everything in life is a risk after all I have so much stake my money on much fake investment platforms in the past base on risk. So I moved two hundred dollars ($200) from my spot wallet into my Binance future wallet. I opened some trades with the little knowledge I gathered so far to my uttermost surprise I was making little profit after the end of my trade because most of the time I use the stop loss and take profit method Also at times I don't use the option, I profit little and I also loose trade at times, I was doing this trial by an error of trading strengthening my skills in trading each day that passes not until in the month of August when my greed drives me to make it big in trading and investing, my heart, my thought began to magnet onto me the things that I was thinking about on how to start making it big in day trading so that I could go into it full time and practically forget of doing any other work. As if my thoughts will engineer my desire because at that period almost all the sponsored adverts I was seeing on social media on Facebook, YouTube, Instagram, and TikTok were all about advertisements of trading and investment of different financial brokers, I was coming across so many adverts on social media about Quantum AI and so many other financial bookers camouflaging to be real and giving proposal in having trading bot that can predict the market accurately without using human emotion and gives out high daily profit returns, they always mention a starting fund capital of two hundred and fifty dollars ($250). Most of these social media-sponsored adverts will show pictures of Elon Musk or Mark Zuckerberg talking about his invention of the Quatum AI trading bot, and many other video tools used for different campaign adverts. Many captivating offers are what they always assure their prospective client who will turn up to sign up on the website. After countless seeing those different sponsored adverts made with different videos, I got attracted to one of the video adverts on YouTube but had also seen the particular video played several times on Facebook, The description of the video is a Man who pulls out from a white Lamborghini flashy car, he said in the video that he has been walking around town looking for someone he will introduces to trading software that can transform his or her financial status, Then a woman passing by him as he excuses the woman demanding just a two minutes of her time but the woman declined stating that she is already late for work, the Man assures her that if she gives him two minutes of her time she may never work again but still the woman declines his statement and walk out from him. Oh gosh for the man he is an engineer and not a salesman so maybe getting someone on the street to introduce a financial platform that is possible of transforming lives will be tougher than he expects, then Another guy across the road echoes at the man complimenting his nice white flashy Lamborghini car, do you want one the man ask him, yes I wish replied the guy across the road, then the man beckon on the guy at the other side of the road to come over for a second, the man with the car introduced himself as Brandon to Jerry the guy at the other side of the road struggling for financial stability, Brandon offers to buy Jerry a drink so that they can have a time together, so at the drinking shop Brandon introduces Jerry to the financial system he created that can generate trading profit while using the trading software. In summary of the video story, Jerry tried out the trading software called Gemini 2 trading App using a minimum of two hundred and fifty dollars as a start-up capital investment in just two minutes the rest is a wonder story as Jerry Henceforth begins to virtually profit in greater profit. so this very particular video get me interested seeing the story wonder of Jerry and I decide to try the website out, I click on the sign up button and registered with my email and password, soon after the registration I started receiving calls from a lady using London dial code saying to be my account manager, the lady told me to activate my account and trade with the robot but that I need to fund my trading account with the minimum of two hundred and fifty dollars ($250), at first after receiving the call I thought it wise in my mind to back off from this business deal remembering my previous wrong encounters with other wrong sites, but this very lady keep disturbing me with her frequent countless calls that I later decided to give it a try, I transfer two hundred and fifty dollars ($250) from my Binance wallet account, they say all sort of mouth watering promises that I wouldn't remembered to mentioned but in all they said the few words I could remembered was that the trading bot will be giving ninety percent correct market technical analysis and an expert trader will be assign to me to be helping me forecasting the market trends. They later promised a fifty percent return on profit at the end of weekly trade. Later on, I was trading together with the expert trader they assigned to me, I later asked them about the trading bot they mentioned earlier to be doing the trading but they said that the human trader they assigned to me was more capable of handling the trading that using trading bot most at times causes inefficiency and inaccuracy but using human knowledge and judgment to execute trades is far better because of human logical thinking. I was first trading with Barckely Stone or BR Stone as their name implies with an initial two hundred and fifty dollars as trading capital, Later on, my human greed played on me again as I thought it wisely to expand my investment with others financial bookers I discovered as well on social media, I sign up with Xtr Trade, and IG Phoenix. I deposited two hundred and fifty dollars with IG Phoenix but I was tricked into depositing three thousand three hundred dollars ($3,300) with Xtr Trade because the man assigned to me as my trade assistant used Anydesk Application to hack through my Binance wallet and transferred out from my wallet the sum of three thousand three hundred dollars into the trading dashboard they created for me as my trading account I question him for the wrong action why he will move such amount of money out from my Binance spot wallet to the trading account he created for me using their website instead of the initial two hundred and fifty dollars ($250) as the start-up capital which I agreed to deposit, but he said he wanted to trade big with big start-up capital and he assures that I get bigger profit weekly, but I told him I never give him the right to move out all the money in my Binance wallet out without my consent. These guys will use the App called Anydesk to manipulate one phone and laptop and gain access. They asked me to share my system with them using Anydesk Application so that they could assist me in doing the trading but more of an intention for them to manipulate my system. I told him I want to pull back the money he pulled out from my Binance wallet without my consent he tried everything possible way to convince me not to bother pulling back the money but I refused, that was when I began to sense that these social media financial bookers are not who really I thought they are, I began to sense it that they nothing but scam. Moreover during the cause of my trading with these social media financial brokers I open a separate private Forex account with Axis using MetaTrader 4 trading App to trade Forex on my own but using the trading signals these guys that called themselves trading experts to open trade but I found out that the trading signals they are forecasting is seventy-five percent (75%) poor trading signal in the sense the market will always go against their analysis causing me to be liquidated twice. I threatened to report their company to the Financial Conduct Authority (FCA) after I made the threat message that was the end with Xtr trade bookers for they stopped communicating with me, I wrote to them several times but I got no reply from them, not too long after my encounter with Xtr trade the other two bookers IG Phonix and BR Stone start urging me to increase my initial capital deposit so that I can be earning much profit, I replied the two bookers why will I increase my capital deposit when I have not received any trading profit from them so far, they try all their best to sweet talk me into upgrading my trading account with some thousands of dollars I bluntly declined their sweet talk and demand a withdrawal from my profit they made so far after three months of trade. They perceived that my heart had been made up and not ready to release any penny for an upgrade. First IG Phonix stopped communicating with me few weeks later BR Stone liquidated my account and stopped communicating with me too. I wrote to FCA about my encounter with these three financial bookers I invested my money but FCA replied stipulating that there is nothing they can do to help me because they are not licensed financial bookers in the UK and for that, they are not regulated meaning they can't be traced to be persecuted by the law, they are just bunch of scammers ripping off innocent people their earned money.

## WISE INVESTOR:

Here I have started a clear story of my encounter with these fake bookers parading their dubious advert on almost all social media, Their target social media are Facebook, Instagram, and YouTube. You might have come across most of these fake marketing tools of different kinds of videos claiming to have a trading bot that can help you trade making a huge profit and all manner of money doubling trading bot or having an expert financial trader that will be your trading guide, majority of those adverts are fake, desist to fall a trap with them, I am a victim of their skillful scam and I wouldn't like any other person to fall a victim. You might be seeing a video advert of Elon Musk or Mark Zuckerberg talking in the video, It is a clown video advert so don't think is the real Elon Musk or Mark Zuckerberg talking. They call their prospective client with ultimate persuasion talking in their target into the trap of promising awesome packages of higher return of investment profit.

If you want to entrust your money with any financial broker for investment or copy trading make sure that you have research about that firm and make sure that the financial booker is regulated so that if anything negative should happen with your money you can easily report the company to financial authorities so they can take up the matter and help you recover your fund. There are many financial brokers with legal licenses to operate, Research about these legit financial brokers and invest with them. I repeat again do not invest your money with any financial broker that the company is not regulated because it is a game of risk and you can wake one day only to discover that your whole money is gone.

And finally, I keep on saying avoid greed in investment, Greed is a deadly poison of financial destruction when it comes to investment, don't invest with greed in your heart and in your head.

You might as well have seen a sponsored advert on social media mostly on Facebook, YouTube, and Instagram claiming to be a Law Agency or whatever name as Financial crime control agency promising to recover your money from all these online scammers ranging from one thousand dollars ($1000) and above, they will provide a site link where you will sign up with your email and phone number. Don't fall for such scams because they are all scammers in different categories, The First category of these scammers are the ones proposing you invest or trade with them to help maximize your profit, The second category of these scammers might be proposing to have a trading software to sell to you that will help you to make more trading profit. The last category of these scammers are the ones that propose to help recover your scam money. These are all the same scammers projecting malicious offers in different categories, they are smart scammers of the twenty-first century so desist from listening to them, don't fall for their malicious trap, and lose every connection you have with them if you are already engaged with them. At times these scammers write you through email using email marketing methods to promote their malicious act claiming that they will help you recover your lost money from scam sites don't give them the space to come into your life, be quick to block them off. In this internet era, I sincerely advise that it is very important to have basic knowledge of cyber security because it will help you a lot to protect your data, information, and funds from internet intruders daily creating baits, and phishing for people to be trapped.

## 2023 THE FOOLISH INVESTOR BECOMES THE WISE INVESTOR

After the biggest scam in the year 2022 with the social media financial brokers I called myself to caution and advised myself with all seriousness, I buried my greed, and I flushed the thought of "Sleep, wake, and see money" from my mind which was the origin and architect that birth out all my misfortune in my quest of trading and investing.

But now the once foolish investor is now a wise investor, experience they say is the best but bitter learning, My rough experience and my mistakes in the financial market have really become a lifetime financial lesson to me in trading and investing that I can never forget anytime, it is an indelible memory in my head. I now trade with caution and experience; I now only invest in the best stocks and tokens with best future potentials using the best Crypto exchange Apps and invest with best regulated financial brokers. My experience is really a teacher and that is why I took my time to document my foolish mistakes in the book so that any new investor that comes across this text will learn from this series of serial mistakes I made. Trading and investment are encouraging and good if only should be done wisely. I have given out all the advice I am familiar with during the cause of my trading and investment mistakes but there is one thing I will repeat over again which is,

Be careful with your thoughts and what you wish for, your thought is really a strong striking force that can make you in life or instead mar you in life, I have heard many lectures earlier about the willpower of thought, and read some books about it but I never really take it seriously not until I became a victim of my own weak thought. In truth, I am sincere enough to confess that what really dragged me into the financial market unprepared is my constant ill thought of "Sleep, wake, and see money" The thought not only pushed me into the financial market unprepared but also awakened the human greed lying calmly in me before. I will advise again, discard any negative thoughts you have in mind, guide your thoughts as a man will guide his treasure room with a gun, and Delete now the filthy thoughts you already have in mind.

**CAUTION:** Should in case as the cause of you reading the storyline of this book and get infuriated with an anger of what kind of person I am that makes mistakes like this with money repeatedly, please I will first ask you personally for forgiveness and beg you not to get mad at my many foolish mistakes. I repeat again, In case you are reading the book and bitterly keep wondering in your mind what kind of a person is this that repeatedly makes mistakes like this please permit me to create a fresh reminder for you to please pause a while from reading and turn at the back cover of the book and console your angry heart with the title of the book.

**Cheers...**